SOUL ON FIRE

Randy Fox

Table of Contents

Dedication

My soul is on fire for my wife Marne.

This book is dedicated to you for your love, support and continual encouragement to pursue my passions.

I love dreaming and dancing through life with you.

Foreword

It is my honor to present the book, *Soul on Fire,* to you. It is written by a young man, Randy Fox, whose name you will be hearing about for years to come in the area of corporate motivation and excellence.

I tell you this because I have just read his first book, which captures the power of passion, the love of leadership, the methodology of motivation and the essence of excellence.

These four entities are the Mt. Rushmore of success in any profession. Randy has not only highlighted them for us, he has examined them, explained them and expressed them with enthusiasm, inspiration and honesty giving the book a real chance to be a memorable classic someday.

Soul on Fire is not a book you scan and shelve or one that politely piques your interest. It will grip your soul to the point where you will see yourself nodding in agreement with its principles and wanting to turn the next page to add a dimension to your potential you may have never known existed before.

It is filled with inspirational quotes, insightful *FoxPoint* bullets on leadership and life, and poignant stories that will make you laugh and make you cry.

In these pages you will discover the joy and personal intimacy of your Impossible Dream, finally believing it can actually come true. You will be driven to Improve Yourself in ways you had never realized before now.

You will learn the Communication Cues of body language, tone of voice and facial expression to give you a power edge not only in business, but also in relationships, and all of life.

The chapters roll on stimulating your mind and firing up your soul, as you understand the life-changing gift of Dispensing Hope to those who need to smile again, and the unselfishness you can experience in Making Others Successful, which multiplies your effectiveness as well as your legacy.

Randy begins *Soul on Fire* by stressing the importance of Loving Leadership if we are to respect the power of the position and use it to make a difference in our world.

He ends with Persistence, which defines the difference between great leaders like Anthony Robbins and John Maxwell and the wannabes who lack the fire in their indecisive soul and burn out along the way.

This book is not for the faint of heart. It is a challenge for you to not just understand the art of leadership but to allow it to grab you, to let it stoke the hot fires of passion within you to make your life count for something.

Or, as Randy Fox says over and over again, "find your dream and help others find theirs, too."

My hope is that you will not just buy the book but **become** the book. I promise you will not regret it, for your life will never be the same again.

Believe it.

The world is waiting for you.

Patrick Hurley
Author and Emmy-award winning Producer

February 14, 2014

Prologue

The Importance of Passion

A fifth-grade boy was talking to his friends one day who told him about the upcoming Christmas card selling contest at their elementary school. The boy absorbed the information and enthusiastically announced, "I'm going to win first prize!"

His two classmates were skeptical. The boy was new at the school and he didn't have many friends. They laughed at his boast.

For the next several weeks, the fifth-grader went door-to-door with the sales pitch he had written, "Hi, I go to St. Anthony's Grade School and we are selling Christmas cards to send money to sick children all over the world. Would you like to buy a box, it's only a dollar?"

Some days, the little boy would sell as many as three boxes, most days he would sell none. But every day, as soon as he got home from school he would change his clothes, put his boxes in his bicycle basket and pedal through the neighborhood.

His mom was concerned on some of those days, "Honey, it's raining outside." Her son would respond, "I want to win!" Another time she would say, "You have a bad cold!" He would smile, "I want to win!" She even enticed him, "We're all going out for ice cream!" He laughed, "I want to win!"

His main competitor, who had won every year, was a year older. His strategy was much simpler, he would put out all his boxes on a Sunday morning after church and his relatives bought the entire case. That's how he won.

But, the younger lad, despite doing it the hard way was closing in on him. With Christmas Day approaching, he was only one box short of victory. His teacher extended the deadline and on the last day of the contest, the little boy sold two boxes and WON!

No one could believe it.

He had done it!

The young boy had made good on his promise to win.

Did he win because he had a better plan? No.

Was he successful because he had the right connections?

Not at all.

Did he come in first place because he had the most experience?

Absolutely not.

What was his secret?

He had *passion*.

He wanted first place more than anything else in the world.

He had the will to win.

Passion: def. "Passion is when you put more energy into something than is required to do it. It is more than just enthusiasm or excitement, passion is ambition that is materialized into action to put as much heart, mind, body and soul into something as is possible." *Urban Dictionary*

It is more than something you are good at, more than enjoyment. It is the total abandonment for what you love. It is a strong desire that you cannot quench unless you are doing that.

That little boy taught us that this is not about age, experience, know-how, talent, background, culture or brash talking.

It's about the soul.

Big boys understand passion, too. Like Jack Welch, the former CEO of General Electric, the parent company of NBC Television, stated:

"The world will belong to passionate driven leaders, people who not only have enormous amounts of energy but who can energize whom they lead. In all my years of observing people, I have yet to meet an individual who reached his potential but didn't possess passion."

You want to reach your potential?

Possess passion.

You want to grow as an organization?

Possess passion.

You want maximum performance?

Possess passion.

A leader loves passion.

This book is on leadership.

Specifically, the *passionate* loves of a Leader.

Let's get started.

Chapter One

Dreaming the Impossible Dream

We kick things off with the core of my soul, for I believe in the Dream.

"I love those who yearn for the impossible."
Goethe

Let me tell you about my only sibling, my younger brother, Steve.

One day when I was in high school, we went to see the movie, *Hook,* starring Dustin Hoffman and Robin Williams. The hook part explains why pirates always seem to have an eye patch. My guess they forgot they were wearing one when their eyes itched.

Memory is important.

After the movie, my brother couldn't stop talking about the music composer and conductor, John Williams, of *Hook*.

He told me, "That's what I want to do with my life. I want to lead an orchestra like him."

Steve was in the sixth grade.

Most of his friends wanted to be policemen or firefighters or be a running back for the Bears.

My brother wanted to be a maestro.

Really?

For the next several years, that is all my brother talked about, "I want to conduct an orchestra." He did play in the college band but no one really believed he would go beyond that in his life.

He had a dream. Most people, including his family and close friends called it, "An Impossible Dream."

Most people were dead wrong.

It happened on the day, Steve and his wife, Leslie, packed up all their stuff and moved from Wheaton, IL to Los Angeles, CA.

Why?

Because Steve Fox wanted to be an orchestra conductor.

My dad was dumbfounded. He tried to be practical, "Son, you have very little money, you don't know anyone in LA and you have no experience being a conductor..."

Crazy.

A crazy dream.

Today, my little brother is the founder and conductor of the Golden State Pops Orchestra in Southern California.

I am so proud of him.

He even met John Williams on several occasions and told him how Mr. Williams had influenced his career.

I remember that day at the movie.

I saw a creepy Captain and a scary crocodile, while my brother saw his Dream. One of us saw a film, the other one saw his future.

His "Impossible Dream" carried him all the way to LA.

Never underestimate the power of your Dream. If you believe it, you will become it.

"**Nothing is impossible, the word itself says 'I'm possible'!**" *Audrey Hepburn*

Pursuing your Impossible Dream is like being a child at Disneyland. It is magical and it takes a great deal of innocence.

It is difficult for a jaded realist to believe in impossible dreaming. He or she sees too many practical pitfalls in attaining it and winds up settling for a modest goal within reason.

It takes a child, or an adult who believes like a child, to ignore the reality and go after the unattainable. That's when dreams come true.

Remember the 1980 U.S. Hockey team?

I can still hear Al Michaels screaming, "Do you believe in MIRACLES, yes!"

Those kids got on the ice and jumped all over the Soviet skaters. They out sped them, out muscled them, out thought them and beat them.

How?

They were naive enough to believe they could do it.

Life is not always about facts and figures that lay a safe path to your destiny. Sometimes, you have to dream beyond what everyone tells you is possible and discover your passion.

"Some of the world's greatest feats were accomplished by people not smart enough to know they were impossible." *Doug Larson*

Ask the Wright Brothers if it made sense to build a vehicle that could actually fly.

Ask a young woman, at a Baltimore television station in 1983, if she believed she would become the most influential woman in the world someday; and Oprah Winfrey would have smiled and said, **"That was my Dream."**

Listen to the heart of Dr. Martin Luther King here from 1963,

"Let us not wallow in the valley of despair, I say to you today, my friends. And so even though we face the difficulties of today and tomorrow, I still have a dream. It is a dream deeply rooted in the American dream. I have a dream that one day this nation will rise up and live out the true meaning of its creed: 'We hold these truths to be self-evident, that all men are created equal.'"

Dr. King never lived to see his dream come true. He died doing everything he could to see it fulfilled. But, he believed in the impossible. He had the childlike faith to express his heart and soul to America and he gave his life for his Dream.

Dreamers don't care about the odds against them. They only trust the greatness before them.

My wife and I took our three children to Disneyland. Our two year-old daughter lit up when she saw all the characters walking around the park. She hugged Minnie and Pluto and any Toon she saw; she *believed* they were real.

The faith and ebullience of a child swept her through Disneyland that day.

We need that same faith.

Don't spend all your time on the reality of why your Dream is not possible, step outside the box and make it happen. Anyone can talk themselves out of trying. It takes a passionate leader to set their face like a flint to realize their Dream.

What value is there in living a life that is not worth dying for?

Ask Martin Luther King.

Ask my brother, Steve.

Ask yourself.

"A negative mind will never give you a positive life." *Ziad K. Abdelnour*

You may be thinking, "What has stopped me from achieving my Impossible Dream?"

From personal experience, I have a few answers for you.

My dream was to stop working for a company in the corporate world and become a successful entrepreneur. I had a passion to motivate others, make them successful and build a career around making a difference in the world.

So, what stopped me from my Dream?

There were several factors that held me back.

The first one was the reality of financial stability. I had a wife and a young child. Leaving a stable, well-paying job was not a reasonable goal for me as I considered a new career as my own boss. At that time in my life, there was too much reality for me to deal with here.

Secondly, I did not have the foundational support of family and friends to undertake a risky move. I needed them to say, "You can do it, Randy!" Their validation was important to me. Instead I received, "You need to provide, have a stable job, work hard, remain loyal and get promoted."

I also didn't want to fail. Like anyone else, I preferred the sweetness of success not the stigma of failure. I lacked the experience of understanding how to succeed as an entrepreneur. I needed more experience, more work, more time.

I wasn't innocent enough to hurl myself into the biggest wave in oceanic history and shout, "Cowabunga!" and go for it.

"The only place where your dream becomes impossible is in your own thinking."
Robert H. Schuller

At that point in my life, my self-doubts outweighed my Impossible Dream.

Then, the tide began to turn. There was a shift in my thinking.

I was the assistant plant manager in Clinton, Illinois. As I shared my dream to a co-worker named Sharon, I said, "I want to be one of those people who is teaching and motivating others."

She said, "You'd be awesome at that! Why don't

you do it?"

I remember thinking to myself, "I'm going to do it."

After additional promotions and chasing other peoples' dreams for me, my life was rattled. My wife was diagnosed with an incurable cancer.

Cancer.

Pain.

An analysis of what was *really* important. And what mattered.

When she passed away in late 2006, I promised myself to stop getting trapped in the rat race. To make sure my time, efforts and work were maximized with people I cared for, and to fulfill my dream.

My dream.

To help others succeed in life.

That was it.

That was the day I became an innocent child again.

"We would accomplish many more things if we did not think of them as impossible."
Vince Lombardi

I will caution you. There will be people in your life

that will not be supportive of any major changes in your career. You may even be married to one of them.

But, following your Dream is not a popularity contest or the result of a focus group. This is soul-driven. If you believe in it, you are a majority of One.

One of my heroes is Jim Valvano, the late, great basketball coach at North Carolina State University. He had a habit of writing his goals down on note cards. He would jot his dream down, usually Impossible, and relentlessly pursue it. He wanted to marry a certain girl and she became his wife. He wanted to win a National Championship in basketball and his 1983 Wolfpack team accomplished it.

Then, he contacted back cancer. The doctors gave Jim Valvano very little chance of surviving it.

He took out a note card and wrote, "Beat cancer."

He lost that battle.

But, his inspiring words live on when it comes to the Impossible Dream. In his last major speech at the ESPY awards he expressed the essence of following your passion:

"Ralph Waldo Emerson said, 'Nothing great could be accomplished without enthusiasm,' to keep your dreams alive in spite of problems whatever you have. That is the ability to be able to work hard for your dreams to come true, to become a reality."

Then he concluded with the words that will always be his mantra:

"Don't give up, don't ever give up."

That is the heartbeat of every Impossible Dreamer. Those are your words to live by as you pursue your lifelong passion.

Several lessons for you here:

Write everything down

Put your Dream on paper along with everything else that goes to make it a reality. Reading it over and over will set your passion in stone.

Don't be a realist

Dare to use your imagination over your intellect.

Stop listening to your critics

Don't count your critics, weigh them. Most of the people you know are status quo realists. It is understandable they will not approve of any change in your life and career that moves away from there.

It was once stated, "When someone tells you that you can't do something, perhaps you should consider that they are only telling you what they can't do."

Make failure your friend

Coming up short is not your enemy, it is your teacher. Learn from the mistakes you make and re-adjust your tracks as you lay them down anew. An aborted or failed Dream is never a failure. It is teaching you to lay down the right tracks which you may not get right the first time.

The successful lubricant, WD-40, is so named because the owner failed 39 times before it worked on the next attempt. He finally found his Impossible Dream.

Become a child again

Innocent, naive, always believing you can accomplish anything and unaware of the odds against you. Don't let any negative thoughts or facts clutter up your magical approach to finding your Dream.

"Don't give up, don't ever give up."

If you are to have a great legacy, start and end with these words.

"If you choose not to pursue your dreams, you'll still be a part of a dream - only it will be someone else's." *Mike Hawkins*

The title of my book is not a mistake, it is my mission.

Soul on Fire is about leadership, passion, motivating others, being unselfish, and using your spiritual side to make a difference in the world and finding your Impossible Dream.

This is my heart.

I was in the corporate world for years and I did good work there. I always supported my companies and their goals.

Now, I am supporting my Dream and its impact on the world.

That is your decision, to be part of your Dream or someone else's goals. I believe life is short.

Pursuing my Impossible Dream.

It is the greatest way to live a life.

The Dream is who we want to be.

 "We are happiest when we live our Dream."

Dream: def. A gratifying and excellent condition or achievement that is longed for; a beautiful aspiration.

A final thought.

As a leader you love the Impossible Dream because you need to teach your followers to love it, too.

We cannot pass on what we have never experienced.

The world does not need a few Impossible Dreamers, it needs millions of them. Because the world needs to be changed for the better.

I wish there were a Disneyland in every state, every country.

"Consult not your fears but your hopes and your dreams. Think not about your frustrations, but about your unfulfilled potential. Concern yourself not with what you tried and failed in, but with what it is still possible for you to do."
Pope John XXIII

I dream there will be thousands who read this chapter and become an Impossible Dreamer.

I want to make a difference in my life, *and,* I dream of making a difference in yours, too.

Will you join me in a childlike quest to imagine greatness here?

Let's enjoy, **The Happiest Life on Earth!**

Chapter Two

Leadership

Let's begin by defining the word, leader.

Leader: def. "One who *leads*."

Don't let the simplicity fool you.

Most leaders don't lead.

The first question you must ask yourself, "Do I want to live my life as a leader or as a follower?" Make a decision here. You cannot function as both.

Here is a great quote about a politician from the French Revolution who was clueless about being a leader.

"There go my people. I must find out where they are going so I can lead them."

He was a follower of people, not a leader of them.

Our society today is dominated by social networking, reality television stars, negativity and a lack of general respect for others and even ourselves.

This means we listen to others too much, care about their opinions, are immersed in a shallow and negative culture and tend to give up easily when the going gets tough.

That is why our nation lacks real leadership. Think about it.

Our leaders have been replaced by *politicians.* That is not real leadership.

We need real leaders today. Or we will eventually die out as a nation.

Don't just believe me, look at history. The Greek and Roman Empires along with several other dynasties all fell from *within.* That is our fate if we continue on our present course.

The world is starving for great leaders. We need you to build your life as a leader. The first step in that is for you to love being one. Loving leadership also means loving the following:

To make a difference in the world

A leader is interested in making a difference. They aren't huddled within their status quo and protecting their own interests.

"The purpose of life is not to be happy. It is to be useful, to be honorable, to be compassionate, to have it make some difference that you have lived and lived well."

Ralph Waldo Emerson

Your life was never designed to be selfish. What good is a life that is not worth dying for? Is life all about making a salary, having a family, retirement and social security benefits?

There is a world out there that needs men and women to make a difference in changing it. We are all part of our planet. Let's contribute to it with passionate leadership.

Two black men, Martin Luther King and Mike Tyson. One was selfish with his life; it was all about him. The other gave up his life; it was all about him making a difference.

Which one do you want to emulate?

Martin Luther King dedicated and ultimately gave up his life for his cause and his passion. Mother Teresa lived in poverty to help heal, care for and love the world. For them, it was all about making a difference.

These are leaders you need to emulate.

Here is another motivation of a man or woman, who loves to lead:

To serve people

A great leader loves people.

You aren't leading for you, you are leading for others!

Zappos is one of the best companies today because of their service; they want customers to be happy. They ship UPS (for free) and many times upgrade their services to overnight delivery just to wow their consumers.

One time I purchased shoes online at 11:00 p.m. CST and my shoes arrived at 9:00 a.m. Ten hours after I ordered them they shipped from Kentucky to the Chicago suburbs.

Why?

Because CEO Tony Hsieh built a company that loves people, and that company went from zero in 1999 to $1 billion in just ten years. Check out this quote from him,

"Build honest and open relationships with communication."

The people-centered and passionate leader. That's *how* you build a billion dollar company in just ten years, folks.

Leaders also love:

Change

Status quo people are rarely leaders.

Why?

Because evil never idles, it is always moving downward. In order to fight it, a leader must continually adapt and move strongly with vision, risk and change.

A leader's legacy is seared with adaptation.

He is willing to abandon the status quo.

When Steve Jobs returned to Apple in 1997, the tech company he co-founded more than two decades earlier was on the brink of failure. During the final quarter of 1996, Apple's sales plummeted by 30%.

Jobs realized that Apple had been producing multiple versions of the same product to satisfy requests from retailers. He got to work reducing the number of Apple products by 70 percent.

As a leader committed to adaptation, his risky move paid off.

One year later, the company turned a $309 million profit.

Change.

General Dwight D. Eisenhower boldly chose the shorelines of France on June 6, 1944, a risky decision, and D-Day turned out to be the turning point of World War II.

Change.

In 1803, under President Thomas Jefferson, a major adaptation was made to change the landscape of the United States. It was called, the Louisiana

Purchase, which added 828,000 square miles and eventually fifteen states to our country. It was a huge risk at the time, even questioned as unconstitutional. It shattered the status quo of our nation. Definitely.

Change.

In 1970, Paul "Bear" Bryant invited an integrated football team to Alabama to play his all-white squad. 'Bama lost to USC, 42-17. That loss, which many believe was deliberately orchestrated by Bryant to convince his governor and fans to end segregation, allowed him to begin recruiting black players and dramatically changing the way football was played in the South.

Change.

If you love being a leader, start changing the status quo around you.

The final asset of a person who loves to lead:

Inspiration

A passionate leader loves to inspire and challenge others. That is his mother's milk. Giving people hope, opportunity, motivation and promise is what great leaders do. If you love being a leader you will love impacting the lives of followers.

"If your actions inspire others to dream more, learn more, do more and become more, you are a leader." *John Quincy Adams*

Men and women who love leadership want to be the kind of human beings who raise the potential and position of others. That is why they became leaders in the first place.

In sports, the leaders who make others great are called point guards, pitchers and of course, quarterbacks. They are the ones who lead the way and get things done.

Remember this phrase:

"There are three types of people in this world, those that make things happen, those who watch things happen and those who say, 'What happened?'"

As a leader, you are a "happening maker," not a follower, a spectator or clueless. You are the one who ignites others to move, to engage, to change, to grow, to improve and to become great.

You are the leader because you want to be. You love being the leader. You are a leader because, "You are one who LEADS."

We need authentic, trustworthy, competent men and women that will train and mentor the next generation.

Passionately.

It's time for you to fall in love with being the leader. Always.

The world is waiting for you.

Chapter Three

<u>Dispensing Hope</u>

A Christian speaker was receiving a line of teenagers after he gave his presentation that night and a young man walked up to him, "My name is Roger. I heard you at my school today and I wanted to thank you for saving my life."

The youth evangelist was happy to make a spiritual impact on the young man and he smiled, "Well, I'm glad to see you excited about your new faith."

Roger looked at him and said, "You don't understand. It goes deeper than that..." He rolled up his sleeves and revealed bloody bandages which he lifted off to show fresh slash marks on both wrists. The speaker was stunned.

"I tried to kill myself this morning before school. I was going to finish the job tonight but came to hear you speak instead. My dad always told me I wasn't worth anything. You told me I was. I am choosing life from now on. I am going to be great someday. Thank you, sir."

A leader dispenses hope. He helps people realize their value. In a world that loves to put people down, the leader is committed to building them back up again.

"When the world says, 'give up,' hope whispers, 'try it one more time'."

Roger is not in the minority. There are millions of people who feel down about themselves and the lack of success they enjoy.

If you don't believe me, try to compliment someone and see how they respond to it. Instead of beaming with appreciation you will hear responses like, "Oh, you're just being nice," "Flattery will get you nowhere," "If you really knew me you wouldn't say that," "Okay, what do you want?" and so on.

Sad, huh?

Why do so many of us lack esteem? Why do we focus on our negative traits rather than the positive ones?

There are several reasons beginning with the way many of us were raised...

Most parents and grandparents came from a generation of, "Talk's cheap and it's what you do that counts." They were not enamored with words, but by actions. They also were not prone to being complimentary, either.

If you came home from school with all B's and one C grade, your dad might ignore all the good marks and focus on the one negative. "Why'd you get a C?"

If you came home the following semester with all B's he might respond, "I don't see any A's."

If you got A's and B's he still would remain unsatisfied, "If you can get A's in some of your classes, you should get A's in all of your classes!"

You finally get all A's and his "compliment" might be, "What took you so long?"

That doesn't build self-esteem, it negates it.

So, as an adult when someone tells you, "You did a great job!" You become your dad and respond, "It was far from perfect" and put your performance and yourself down.

Welcome to someone who resists hope.

After a number of those experiences, it is difficult to sustain personal significance.

This is the leader's challenge, to redo damage that has been done over a lifetime to so many people in our society today.

Other reasons why people need hope could be, a genetic disposition towards negative thoughts and behavior, depression caused by trauma, financial problems, criminal activity leading to incarceration, a painful divorce, a loss of a loved one, losing one's job and a shameful addiction.

And, a hundred more reasons.

People out there need a lot of hope to smile again.

"Few people are successful unless other people want them to be." *Charlie Brown*

A true story about an eight year-old child actor.

He was rehearsing in a cable television comedy special and he kept forgetting his lines. His confidence was eroding. The show's producer stopped the scene and brought the lad out into the hallway to talk to him. He asked the boy, "Do you want to be an actor or not?

The kid replied, "Uh, yeah. I'm just having trouble remembering my lines." The producer shook his head, "No, you are not trying hard enough. You keep talking to your friends, running up and down the hallways and not focusing here. Do you want me to find someone else for this part?"

The boy said, "No. I want this."

The producer said, "How badly do you want it?"

The youngster looked at him in the eye and said, "Badly."

"Okay," said his mentor, "Get back in there and show me."

"Sir," the boy asked, "Do you think I will be a good actor someday?"

The producer shook his head, "Someday, no. I think you are a good actor NOW."

The lad beamed with excitement, "Wow!"

They went back inside and the young actor did his lines perfectly. He made the comedy show a success.

But, that's not the end of the story...

A year later, that little boy was hired by ABC Television to star in a new sitcom for them. It was called, *The Wonder Years.*

The little boy's name was Fred Savage. He went on to become a star.

All he needed was some hope at an important time in his life.

There are millions of great people out there and they don't even realize it. It is our job as leaders to bring it out in them. We are the dispensers of hope. We turn the switch of the pilot light inside them. They just need that spark.

"The task of leadership is not to put greatness into humanity, but to elicit it, for the greatness is already there." *John Buchan*

Can you remember a time when you made a difference in a person's life encouraging them to be greater just by giving them hope?

Let me suggest an exercise for you.

Start a journal of greatness

Write down moments when you redirected a person's life by giving them hope. Every time you do it, add their name and the story in your journal. Not only will it give you a reminder of what you should be doing as a leader, it will deepen your commitment to serving others.

Wherever you go, look for opportunities to give someone a little hope.

When you think of great people in history what names come to mind?

Abraham Lincoln, George Washington, Franklin Delano Roosevelt, Albert Schweitzer, Dr. Martin Luther King, Mother Theresa, Angelina Jolie, classic names with one thing in common, they all gave people *hope* at a key moment in time.

Whether it was confronting a devastated nation during the Great Depression, freeing black slaves and giving them dignity, giving the colonists the belief they could break away from England or serving the disadvantaged in India, hope abounded whenever these individuals stood up and stood tall for others.

We have had famous people that have been celebrated, too. Men and women like Elvis Presley, Marilyn Monroe, Muhammad Ali, Babe Ruth, the Beatles and so on. But, we need to distinguish the famous from greatness.

Fame is mostly self-centered, greatness is other-centered. As a leader, your goal should not be to serve yourself but to serve others. That is where you will find your legacy. That is also where you will find your joy.

When you become a leader with passion and

a heart for others, you live in a world that is a blessing to you and others wherever you go. That is a universe of personal fulfillment for it brings constant joy and thankfulness with it.

Think about this for a moment, have you ever had someone reach out to you and make a difference in your life because they sensed you needed a kind word, a smile or a hug?

Dispensers of hope. We have all had a few in our lifetime.

I remember one of them.

I was a freshman in high school.

My father was the assistant principal and one of the coaches on the varsity football team. He was respected and well-liked.

As his son, I was not only protected at school, I had a great life there.

Then, my dad filed for divorce and moved out leaving me the eldest man at home with my mom and younger brother.

I was devastated.

My father not only changed our family dynamics, he crushed my world. The sun stopped shining in my life.

As a child of divorce, I lost hope. I had nowhere to turn and no clue how to emotionally function, especially in high school.

Without my dad, I was lost.

If you are from a divorced home, you understand the importance of encouragement in those moments.

I needed hope.

A word, a smile, a pat on the back.

Something.

One day, as I was feeling pretty low, I bumped into a classmate who was on his way to being a star player on our football team. He also happened to be a nice guy and really caring even though everyone worshipped him.

His name was Kent Graham. He greeted me and said, "Hey Fox, how are you doing?"

"Great," I lied.

No matter how we feel when asked that question don't most of us lie?

I started to move past him and he put his hand on my shoulder and said, "I know."

He was referring to my parent's divorce.

I just looked at him like a puppy dog needing a bone.

Kent gave me one, "You're going to get through this, Randy. You're going to be okay."

He made me feel better. He made me smile. He made my day.

I was able to get through a tough time and my freshman year turned out pretty good.

Kent Graham?

He went on to become all-state, played well at Ohio State and went on to be a quarterback in the NFL. Good football player. Wonderful guy.

Great leader.

And, a young man with a heart of encouragement when I needed it most.

As a dispenser of hope you may not turn someone into a superstar but you will turn a sad heart into a smile.

That's what real leaders do.

Every person you meet is a potential candidate for hope. All their life they may have been told negative things or abused or bullied or made to feel insignificant in some way.

 You want to be great? Make someone else great.

You want to better your life? Help someone else better theirs.

The difference between a career and a vocation is a calling. We are not just called to have a job; we are called to express our soul everywhere we go. It is who we are.

45

"There is no more noble occupation in the world than to assist another human being to help someone succeed." *Alan Loy McGinnis*

Remember when you were a little kid in the summertime and it was so hot outside? You were dying from the hot sun. You grabbed a hose and gulped down cold water and then you turned that refreshing coolness on yourself. As the water cascaded over your head and down your body you felt invigorated!

Felt great, huh?

That's what hope does for the human heart. It invigorates it, refreshes it and gives it a second chance. Just like cold water on a humid day, it makes you want to go on.

Hope makes you want to go on.

A leader uses hope to help you feel that way in your life.

I want you to be that leader.

The world is waiting for you.

"The purpose of life is not to win. The purpose of life is to grow and to share. When you come to look back on all that you have done in life, you will get more satisfaction from the pleasure you have brought into other people's lives than you will from the times that you outdid and defeated them.
Rabbi Harold Kushner

Go hook up your hose and find those thirsty people. They need you.

Chapter Four

<u>Improving</u>

"I went to a bookstore and asked the saleswoman, 'Where's the self-help section?' She said if she told me, it would defeat the purpose." *Steven Wright*

Never allow yourself to be content with the gifts and talents you have available to you.

 Complacency is confinement.

A change in our existence is more than just survival.

A case in point.

Jackie was a businesswoman in her late twenties. She had checked into a nice hotel and rented a room for the day. She was not there to sleep; she was there to evaluate her life.

On the surface, things were going well for her. Jackie was one of the top sales reps in her company and was pulling down almost six figures in salary. She was driving a leased car at the company's expense and in line for a 10% raise in the next three months.

In her personal life, Jackie was seeing a man who thought the world of her. He was a successful accountant, had his own firm and was a nice guy. The woman owned a condo in a nice area of her city and had several friends and family members to support her.

Oh, and one other thing.

Jackie was unfulfilled. Something was missing in her life.

She felt trapped. She was not realizing her potential.

Jackie could maintain her life, make lots of money and marry the guy next door. Or, she could make some bold moves that fit who she was and improve her at the risk of taking some huge steps backwards.

It was not an easy decision.

"If you do what you've always done, you'll get what you've always gotten."
Tony Robbins

As she sat at the table in the hotel room, she divided each part of her life into sections. She labeled them, "Career," "Mentors," "Brand," "Home," "Friends," and, "Husband," in that order of prioritization.

Jackie wanted a do-over of her life. She had been heading down a path in her life that was not who she was or what she wanted.

Instead of settling for another ten years of mediocrity, the woman was committed to improving herself and that involved taking some professional and personal risks.

She was not afraid to change her life for the better; in fact she was looking forward to the challenge of it.

She began with her career. Jackie had decided to stop working for someone else and be her own boss. She was going to become an entrepreneur.

To do that, she was going to sell her condo and rent an apartment with a much lower monthly payment. The cash from her condo sale would be reinvested and used as startup costs for her new company.

Jackie had been a great sales rep for her corporate bosses and their goals; it was time to sell for her.

This next step meant finding mentors to educate her on how she could become her own Brand, a unique product that represented who she was and what she offered in the marketplace.

She would even relocate geographically and develop new friends that would match her new life.

It was also time to say goodbye to the man she had been seeing. He was never going to be her husband because she was never going to emotionally settle for second best here, either.

As Jackie sipped her coffee and ate her plate of fruit and veggies, the hours went by. She charted her plan on her laptop and each passing minute brought a wider smile to her face and a deeper peace in her soul.

These feelings and sensations confirmed her decision to improve herself. She was not only on a new track; she was on the right one.

For her.

The quote from Henry David Thoreau no longer applied to her,

"Most men lead lives of quiet desperation and go to the grave with the song still in them."

Jackie had been proactive, had stepped up and changed her life for the better.

A leader is always improving him or her to flow with the changes in life and in their life.

It is the follower who is afraid to leave the status quo which controls him. People will stay in their comfort zones for their entire life rather than discover the beauty they can be.

They ignore the truth that you can only put so much makeup on a pig. Eventually, you need to become a different animal.

Jackie had tired of being a roadrunner. She finally realized she was destined to become an eagle, to soar into the heights of the greatness she had only dreamed about.

She went for a relaxing swim in the hotel pool, enjoyed a lush salad in the dining room, had a manicure and a massage, packed up her computer, checked out of the hotel and as she walked outside, she smiled at the sun that radiated down upon her.

Her first day as an eagle had become a reality.

The mountains and their challenges awaited her. Jackie was excited in a fresh, new way. She had done more than evaluate her life.

She had saved it.

"There is nothing noble in being superior to your fellow man; true nobility is being superior to your former self." *Ernest Hemingway*

Thousands of men and women have improved the quality of their lives in similar ways. It is important to note some of them.

Michael Jordan is considered by many the greatest NBA player in history.

But most people do not know he was demoted from his varsity high school basketball team to the junior varsity. They also don't realize he was an average jump shooter and not a great defensive player, either.

But, MJ changed his game.

He improved his ability by working hard on the areas that held him back as a good player and he became a superstar. His outside shot was responsible for winning playoff games and a couple of NBA Championships.

Over a period of eight years, his team, the Chicago Bulls, won the title six times, a remarkable feat. Without Michael, they wouldn't have won one.

A Hall of Fame NBA coach who won multiple championships with the Lakers echoed this truism,

"Excellence is the gradual result of always striving to do better." *Pat Riley*

What are ways you can improve yourself?

Here are some suggestions:

Examine successful people

I read books like: *The One Minute Manager, 21 Irrefutable Laws of Leadership, Beyond Talent, From Good To Great, The Purpose Driven Life, Who Moved my Cheese, See you at the Top, The Spirit to Serve: Marriott's Way* and so on.

Why?

Because I wanted to learn all I can about people, leadership and success. I was willing to make any changes in my life and career to be better as a person and in my career. I believed books like this would help me get a step closer to excellence.

It can't hurt, right?

If you want to improve, open your mind and be willing to accept as much help as you can so you never get into a rut in life.

Click on keywords and phrases like, "success tips," "improving yourself" and, "habits of effective leaders," etc.

Go to the business section of your local bookstore and browse. Let others do the work for you. Your job is to hear what they have to say and then incorporate it in your life.

"Man only learns in two ways, one by reading, and the other by association with smarter people."
Will Rogers

Hone your expertise

You are good at something, creatively expand it and make it ***better***. Learn all you can about your talent and how to market it in a variety of ways.

More ways to use your talent = A more satisfying life, career, and potentially more money.

If you don't believe me, check out Steve Martin's professional life.

He began as a comedy writer on, *The Smothers Brothers Comedy Hour* in 1967. He could have stayed in Hollywood as a successful writer for the remainder of his career.

Nope.

He wanted to improve himself.

"Every man has in himself a continent of undiscovered character. Happy is he who acts as the Columbus to his own soul." *Sir J. Stephen*

Steve Martin created a unique new Brand for his act and became, "A Wild and Crazy guy!"

He became one of the most renowned stand-up comedians on the planet but he didn't stop there.

Steve taught himself how to become one of the finest banjo players in the world, starred in his first successful movie, *The Jerk*, and went on to make over forty movies, including popular hits, *Parenthood*, *Planes, Trains and Automobiles*, *Roxanne* and, the poignant, *Father of the Bride* movies.

He didn't stop there.

His self-improvement continued as he became a wine connoisseur, owner of some of the finest collections of art, a popular writer, a Grammy winner and the host for the Academy Awards.

He is truly an amazing and remarkable human being not just because he had a great talent for humor but because he multiplied himself in so many ways into so many areas of excellence.

That needs to be you.

Never be satisfied with what you are doing, rather be stimulated by what you can still achieve.

The secret to individual greatness is not what you are capable of doing but by what you are willing to try beyond it.

Here is another key to improving yourself,

Develop advisors and mentors in your life

Behind every successful person in any field is someone who helped educate, challenge and guide them there. You are no different.

Having an experienced and established counselor guiding you as you lay down the tracks of your career is more than invaluable, it is a must. You can only take yourself so far. Let the wise men and women stretch you beyond your own limits of knowledge and understanding.

Be open to what you can gain from a professional who has been there before you.

Go find your Yoda.

Listen.

Learn.

Improve.

May the Force be with your potential.

Attend Leadership Conferences

Take notes and notes and notes. Let the experts train you. Type their stories, memorize their quotes, incorporate their experiences into your mind, feel their passion in your soul.

Every conference you go to will take you one step closer to maximizing your potential as a leader.

Further your trade

Go back to school and get an advanced degree in either your current field of expertise or a new area you want to develop in the future.

Never stop growing.

I know this from personal experience. I used to be a really lousy manager.

Many years ago, I had an employee who was constantly late to work. I tried to have a conversation with her about her tardiness to no avail. I couldn't get anything across to her.

She continued being late.

I was doing something wrong but I had no clue what I was lacking here.

Finally, I attended an in-house corporate training conference and I sought out the advice of a plant manager. He listened to the problem I was having with my employee and bluntly said,

"Right between the eyes."

I responded, "Huh?"

He clarified his statement, "You have to look her in the eye and make it CLEAR!"

I immediately recognized instead of addressing the situation and setting expectations with her, I was helping her make excuses for her irresponsible behavior.

The plant manager told me, "Just state it, connect it to the organization and tell her this is an organizational must. Don't make excuses or apologize, simply tell her she is responsible to her company and that is part of her job."

It worked. She was never late again.

I had been flimsy and weak in trying to remedy the situation and because I was concerned about hurting her feelings or being rejected by her, I was constantly letting her off the hook.

I learned a valuable lesson. I incorporated it into my management style and have used it ever since.

"For things to change, you've got to change. For things to get better, you've got to get better." *Jeff Olson*

I had done several things right to improve my career and myself.

I had gone to a leadership conference to learn new ways of doing things.

I had sought out a manager and used him as a mentor.

I had listened to his advice.

I applied his advice.

I have been applying it ever since as a leader.

"The self is not something ready-made, but something in continuous formation through choice of action." *John Dewey*

Don't be complacent.

Always improve.

Have fun with your new life and career.

You'll be glad you did.

Chapter Five

Communication Cues

Two couples were enjoying high tea at a posh hotel in Chicago. One of the men noticed a waitress coming out of the kitchen and commented, "That waitress needs to go home." The other people at the table looked at him oddly. His wife said, "Honey, what are you talking about?"

He smiled, "Her body language reveals how angry she is right now. She should not be around customers." As he spoke, the waitress went back into the kitchen. As she re-emerged, the husband alerted the other three sitting with him, "Watch her carefully, now."

As the two couples observed her, she brushed heavily into a tall palm plant to the right of the kitchen door. His wife said, "Interesting, she hates plants."

The husband laughed, "That is not a plant to her, that is a person. My guess is that represents a man. She is upset with him."

He called the manager over and explained his perceptions of the waitress. The manager waited for her employee to come through the kitchen door.

She nodded knowingly as she saw the waitress slam into the leafy object and commented, "My employee is angry. You were right. She is going through a nasty divorce. Evidently, that palm plant represents her soon to be ex-husband. I'll send her home so she can cool off."

Communication cues.

If you pay attention, you can read anyone.

Let's begin with the research from Albert Mehrabian on communication. Only 7% of all communication is content, the words we say. 55% is face and body language and 38% is tone of voice.

There you have it.

Most people pay attention to the words a person says but the real keys to communication are *non*-verbal. That is where the insights and power are in the message.

It's time to learn the cues that make up 93% of this wonderful way of expression.

"The art of communication is the language of leadership." *James Humes*

This is a fine art, indeed.

A case in point.

During the Watergate investigation, President Nixon was addressing the Associated Press managing editors in Orlando, Florida:

"And I think, too, that I could say that in my years of public life, that I welcome this kind of examination, because people have got to know whether or not their president is a crook. Well, I am not a crook. I have earned everything I have got."

The words were powerful, confident and decisive.

They were also untrue. This speech was given in August, 1973, over a year before Nixon resigned for trying to cover-up the Watergate break-in. But, if you watch carefully what he does after he makes this declaration you will see that he is guilty well in advance of resigning the Presidency.

He immediately moves back from the podium, slumps down to his left and folds his arms. Guilt, guilt, guilt. He had just lied and he knew it. Body language observers knew it, too.

If you are going to be an effective leader, you need to learn the nuances of communication beginning with the non-verbal signs and tells. Their revelations will profit you both professionally and personally.

In 2005, the movie, "Mr. and Mrs. Smith" opened and the two stars, Angelina Jolie and Brad Pitt were doing publicity to promote the film. When you watch Mr. Pitt speaking, check out the facial expressions and body movements of Angelina Jolie. She keeps looking over at him and flirting with him by the way she is moving.

She was not acting like a professional co-star. She was giving off behavioral signs that she liked him in a romantic sense. A few months after that, the couple announced to the world they had begun dating. Body language experts knew it the day of the press conference.

"When you can read body language, every moment you spend with people you can make it valuable, and if you're in business, you can make it profitable."
Janine Driver, body language expert

We can make this simple, too.

For example, when you are discussing something with a person and they suddenly fold their arms while you are talking, that is bad news. They are putting up a wall.

Change your approach and soften it and chances are good, the arms will come down.

When a woman is on a date and she is stroking her hair on the side with her hands, that is a good sign. It means she wants to kiss her date.

When your conversation partner is standing across from you with their hands clasped behind their head, that is a clear sign they are open and agreeing to your views.

Let's review examples of **facial expression** and how much they give away a person's words.

Paul Eckman, a facial analysis expert developed the seven faces of universal emotion: Happy, Angry, Surprised, Sad, Scared, Disgust and Contempt.

Learn to read these faces. Sit at an airport or a Starbucks and watch the expressions of people as they stand in line or interact with people. Their faces will teach you a lot.

If you are going to motivate others as a passionate leader, you need to be an expert on facial response. It will not only make your job easier, it will benefit you as a professional in the corporate world.

Marion Jones, the world-class sprinter was accused of taking performance enhancing drugs. At her press conference, she defended herself and denied the accusations.

But, there was something revealing in her face as she announced the charges against her were false.

She showed no anger. For a person unjustly accused, Ms. Jones should have been insulted, even defiant.

Nope.

She looked sad and defeated, like a victim.

Her attitude was, "Poor me, why is everyone picking on me?" It was the wrong emotional reaction for an innocent person.

Later, she came out of the courthouse for being convicted of lying to federal prosecutors about taking the drugs and finally admitted the truth. This time, her facial expression reflected genuine sadness.

The face and eyes do not lie.

The remaining 38% of effective communication is realized in **tone of voice**. Here are some cues for you.

Imagine you are driving home with your wife after spending the evening with her parents. She is unusually quiet during the ride. You finally turn to her and ask her, "Are you okay?"

Her answer comes back, **"I am fine."**

Listen carefully to her tone of voice.

C-a-r-e-f-u-l-l-y.

How did she say the word, "fine?"

The texture and tone will tell you her true feelings. If she said it warmly, she is fine. If she said it matter of fact she is fine.

If she responded with an edge of anger or frustration in her tone, she is the opposite of fine. You need to think back over the time you had with her parents to see where you blew it.

Then, be ready to apologize within minutes of asking her, "Why are you upset?"

The word, "fine" is content. The tone of voice is *truth*.

It's not what a person says; it's how they say it.

Remember when you were a child and your mom called you to the kitchen, "Come in here." Remember how her voice immediately told you if you were in trouble or not?

Or your teacher in school says, "See me after class." Check out their tone of voice.

Maybe your employer drops by your desk and states, "I need to see you in my office." His tone will tell you a lot, if you are about to get a raise, be fired or somewhere in between.

I usually talk in a very energetic and loud tone. Excited. Fast. Motivating.

I remember a time when I had to deliver bad news to a client. We all have to do this in our lives. Share something that we know the other person will not like to hear.

I started by speaking slower. I used a softer and lower tone. I was empathetic to their situation and stated that "I know you aren't going to like to hear this, I wouldn't either."

I then went on to share the news.

My message was hard to hear, yet my delivery was soft. I was gentle. They felt my care for them in my voice and thanked me for the call, my honesty and my partnership.

Tone of voice, it is like light in a room, it sets the mood.

Tone of voice is critical to leaders and how they approach their followers. Especially, in politics. Three dynamic speakers as Presidents used their voices to become memorable.

John F. Kennedy spoke in a staccato style with a parallel sentence structure, "Let us never negotiate out of fear, but let us never fear to negotiate," or, "Ask not what your country can do for you, ask what you can do for your country."

Ronald Reagan, a consummate actor who knew how to dramatically read lines used his voice at the end of a tactful, warm and common sense sentence to *dramatically* raise his voice at the end and make his powerful declaration:

"There is one sign the Soviets can make that would be unmistakable, that would advance dramatically the cause of freedom and peace. General Secretary Gorbachev, if you seek peace, if you seek prosperity for the Soviet Union and Eastern Europe, if you seek liberalization, come here to this gate. Mr. Gorbachev, open this gate. **Mr. Gorbachev, tear down this wall!**"

Nice, nice, nice...**BOOM!**

Ronald Reagan knew the power of voice.

Barack Obama uses a sing song, rhythmic delivery that makes him very likeable to his audience. When you listen to him speak, you want to invite him over to your backyard barbecue. His voice is soothing, charming and kind.

Politicians who have run for the Presidency who lacked a powerful speaking voice with inflections and clarity did not win the office. They included, Stevenson, McGovern, Ford, Mondale, Dole, Perot, Kerry, McCain and Romney.

Most of them had a nasal or boring speaking voice that failed to captivate voters.

Tone of voice is critical to a leader.

Learn how to utilize your voice both personally and from a stage. People in the 21st Century want and need to be inspired to greatness. The employees or clients you are called upon to manage and motivate need to be swayed persuasively and they also need a powerful direction.

"The goal is to provide inspiring information that will lead people to action."
Guy Kawasaki

Here are some personal communication cues for you to be aware of on your job and at home:

Mind reading

We assume too much. Never assume you know what your conversation partner is thinking or that they are reading your mind, too. It is always wise to ask during the discussion, "What are you hearing from me?" Remember the communication axiom, "Communication is not what you say it is what the other person *hears*."

Use of the word, "I" instead of, "you"

67

When you are making a point, always say the word "I", using yourself as an example of the problem instead of putting them on the defensive. Powerful counseling technique and invaluable in a relationship argument. Book it.

Be gracious

Never come across as the "expert." That is a great way to lose the respect of the person you are talking to and shut down the conversation. Always be suggestive in your remarks, they will be welcomed.

Phrase your comment in a question, not an accusation

Instead of stating, "You went wrong here!" Change it to, "Let's try and figure out what went wrong here." Or, "Let's work together to see how we can improve next time."

When criticizing always build up the person

Every person needs and deserves value even if they make a mistake. It's the 'Smile Sandwich'. Begin with a smile, something they do well and then gently drop in constructive remarks for improvement. Finally close with encouragement and confidence in them as a person. You will find that by building them up they will accept the criticism with more openness.

Let your conversational partner finish their sentence

This mainly applies to men, especially the Alpha male when conversing here. It also is important for mom and dad to use this maxim when talking to their children. As parents, we tend to talk and not listen.

Even if you know what the other person is going to say, let them say it. It means you value them.

Know your audience

Great leaders adjust to their audience. They know that speaking to a seasoned veteran of the industry is not the same as speaking to an entry-level clerk. Their needs are different. Their experiences are different. How they filter what you say will be too.

Check the emotional mood before speaking

Some confrontations or arguments are not advisable if the emotional environment is volatile at the beginning. Wait for a good time to discuss anything sensitive. If you see your conversation partner beginning to lose it, back off and table the discussion for a later time. Remember this, the right conversation at the wrong time is the wrong conversation.

Practice observing people

Become an expert on 93% of the communication technique. You will be far ahead of most of the population at work and in your personal life.

"The way we communicate with others and with ourselves ultimately determines the quality of our lives." *Tony Robbins*

Finally, sometimes in our lifetime we are going to be asked a question or put into a verbal situation that will leave us tongue-tied or at a loss for a good answer. It happens to the best of us. Let me give you five ways to cover yourself if you are in that position.

Go on the offensive

Change the subject, develop a new topic and be aggressive with your new subject matter. An example of this was President Clinton when asked by a reporter if he could think of any examples of, "a successful 'tax and spend' President in the past."

Instead of getting angry or defensive, Clinton confidently replied, "I believe you are assuming I have been a, 'tax and spend' President when that has not been the case at all."

He then went on the offensive to use the question to explain his financial program leaving the reporter in the dust. Brilliant.

Use humor

JFK and Reagan were masters of humor whenever a question pinned them down. One moment they were trapped by a criticism and miraculously they "pulled a humor rabbit out of their hat" and had the questioner laughing.

Self-deprecation

President Bush was in Japan and went to open a locked door in front of cameras detailing his every move to millions of people. He took advantage of an awkward moment by laughing at himself and saying, "I was trying to escape."

He acted like a child which endeared him to everyone there and came through with flying colors.

Stall with a few sentences

If you are stumped by a question, start using extra sentences on the subject while you stall for the right answer. It works beautifully.

Call on someone else in the room for a moment

A great trick here. If you don't know what to say next, call on someone else to say something next. That will get the focus off of you.

The same is true by reversing the question and asking the one who put you on the hot seat by asking them a question right back. Very effective.

A final thought on communication from a highly successful man,

"Developing excellent communication skills is absolutely essential to effective leadership. The leader must be able to share knowledge and ideas to transmit a sense of urgency and enthusiasm to others. If a leader can't get a message across clearly and motivate others to act on it, then having a message doesn't even matter."
Gilbert Amelio

Time to work on your cues.

Thanks for listening.

Chapter Six

<u>Making Others Successful</u>

Tess graduated from college with a degree in Business Management. She was hired by a large company and worked her way up. As she progressed she took notes along the way preparing herself for the responsibility of running her own team someday.

That day finally came when Tess was assigned over fifty people to manage in the area of sales and marketing for the company.

She had to make a choice here. It was the decision to maintain the status quo and keep everyone in place or to revamp the team she was assigned to lead. Tess had made an initial commitment to make others successful once she had arrived at her place of leadership.

But, as she looked at the specific details of her employees she realized many of them lacked the qualities that would make the grade in a successful corporate world setting.

She realized the status quo approach was not going to work.

Tess had a list of non-negotiable assets she was looking for in her team members. They included: communication skills, personal improvement, helping others, dispensing hope, a commitment to teamwork and the most important aspect of all, a *passion for leadership*.

She was looking for men and women who had fire in their soul.

As she looked at the list of people she was inheriting, many of them lacked the skills and fiery intensity to get the job done.

Tess made her move as a leader.

She worked out a deal with several of them to take an early retirement. It freed her up to add dozens of new team members which reflected her philosophy of a successful sales and marketing force.

She went out and hired two types of employees, superstars and teachable men and women who could develop into superstars. She realized that *the quality of her success would depend entirely on the capability of the team* she had assembled here.

She was absolutely right about that truism.

Tess became the talk of the industry with the results she and her team were able to achieve due to the talented group she had assembled here. Needless to say, she was promoted high up inside her company and additionally, she serves as a consultant to new managers coming into the business.

"It is literally true you can succeed best and quickest by helping others to succeed."
Napoleon Hill

There are two critical pieces to making stars out of the people under your care. The first one is a commitment to talent, like Porsche, "there is no substitute for it."

Build your all-star team.

Now, for the second step.

Let's talk sports.

More specifically, greatness in sports.

We come back to the, "Do you believe in MIRACLES?" game.

U.S.A. hockey 4 Soviet Union 3.

Lake Placid, 1980 Olympics.

The coach of that miracle was the late Herb Brooks who was a dedicated *micromanager*. He believed in detail, force fed it to his players and stalked their every move as they prepared to defeat the greatest hockey team in history.

Other noted leaders in sports that shared this approach were Vince Lombardi and John Wooden.

The opposite motivational leadership style is *macro-management*, the philosophy of stepping back and letting team members achieve the dream more so on their own. Prime examples of this kind of coaching leadership include NBA legend Phil Jackson and Tommy Lasorda.

Which style of leadership works best?

It essentially depends on the players of your team.

If you have superstars, as Jackson and Lasorda did, get out of their way and let them shine.

If you have people who need direction, or you have a system you are teaching like Brooks, Lombardi and Wooden, then dog them until they get it. When they do, they will win championships.

Making stars out of people is the goal of a leader but you have to understand what and who you are dealing with or you will fail miserably in your approach.

"Leadership is lifting a person's vision to high sights, the raising of a person's performance to a higher standard, the building of a personality beyond its normal limitations."
Peter Drucker

Your success as a leader is directly related to the success of your people.

A tale of two managers.

A national organization was loaded with talent in personnel. The employees were high performing, gifted and self-starting. For several years their supervisor used his macro-management approach to perfection.

He gave them the freedom to succeed on their own. In basketball referee terms, "he let them play." Because of his philosophy, they were beyond productive. They thrived on the independence granted to them by their boss.

Then, he took a new job with another company and was replaced by a different leader.

A micromanager.

Everything changed dramatically.

The micromanager closely began observing and controlling the work of his employees. In addition, he took the credit for *their* ideas and innovations instead of honoring his high performing people.

He nitpicked at their work, was quick to criticize and treated them like rookies instead of the quality leaders they were.

Within two years, his sales manager left the company followed quickly by several sales reps, the advertising manager and seven other employees. The micromanager was fired.

The profitable company collapsed. It's still in existence today but nowhere near the giant it had been in the industry.

The quality of the leader will reflect the quality of the team.

"The best executive is the one who has sense enough to pick good men to do what he wants done, and self-restraint enough to keep from meddling with them while they do it."
Theodore Roosevelt

The reason most championship teams throughout history are successful is because they are loaded with talent. You can't make chicken soup out of chicken feathers. You have to have the players, folks.

Either you walk into a situation that already has a Michael Jordan, a Shaquille O'Neal or a Kobe Bryant, or you build your players into those superstars.

As a coach, manager or supervisor, if you are going to win, you need quality players under you, in any field from music to politics.

In the corporate area what are the criteria for a great leader?

Here are some how-to's on making others successful.

Be secure in yourself

An insecure, bullying, wanting all the glory kind of individual will never become a great leader. They will always undercut their employees, garner all the attention and rewards and never be unselfish enough to compliment those under them.

Understand the nuances of your situation

Obviously, your company wants results. Understand the vision, what resources you have and the best methodology to get there. This isn't a one-size fits all approach. Adaptation, as we have discussed, is critical to success.

Find the best people you can

Steve Jobs' brilliance went beyond his product lines. He applied his creativity and insights to designing his team. The men and women he hired had to be as great as his vision and the production of it. He found great players to make Apple a winner.

Know your team

The best way to get the maximum performance from your employees is to understand their "buttons," know what makes them tick. Vince Lombardi was a genius at this art. He knew which of his players responded to a pat on the head and which ones needed a kick in the pants. He intimately knew every one of his forty men and how to specifically motivate them. You need to be that good, too.

Raise their expectations and they will meet them

Most people are either brow beaten, under challenged or not taken seriously. If you want greatness in them, believe in them. Give them faith. Create confidence to go further. That will make them realize there are no limits to what they can do.

Fine-tune them as they grow

As the year goes on adjust their workload, find projects that fit them and make personal and professional suggestions to improve their performance.

Little things like time management training, a social media course, a book on great leaders, a specific management conference or just assisting them in overcoming a bad habit can make a tremendous difference.

Praise and celebrate them

Sam Walton, founder of Wal-Mart believed, "Outstanding leaders go out of their way to boost the self-esteem of their personnel. If people believe in themselves, it's amazing what they can accomplish." He was not only intuitive; he followed that maxim to become a millionaire many times over.

It wasn't just the marketing and sales strategy he implemented, it was the way he treated people.

"The growth and development of people is the highest calling of leadership."
Harvey Firestone

Many years ago I was put in charge of a corporate group of 150 employees. I realized I could not effectively lead this size of team and deliver results on my own.

I needed talent.

I needed leaders.

I picked twelve individuals who possessed the qualities that Tess had looked for in her people, beginning with a passion for leadership. I trained them.

I invested my time and passions in them.

The twelve managers I worked with trained the remaining 138 employees, each taking responsibility for their individual team members.

It worked beautifully. The better I trained, empowered and grew my superstars the more successful the others were, and the more effectively our business performed.

Helping others succeed is not just a phrase, it's a leadership reality.

And, a very powerful success story in corporate performance.

"A good manager is a man who isn't worried about his own career, but rather the careers of those who work for him."
H.M.S. Burns

Chapter Seven

Persistence

Have you ever wanted something or someone so badly you would do just about anything to succeed?

I have a very good friend who wanted to make it in Hollywood as an actor and a comedian. As you know, the odds of success in the entertainment industry are almost impossible. But, my friend had a dream and he realized he would need more than talent to accomplish it.

Five thousand wannabe actors come to Hollywood every month and just as many actors exit Hollywood every month. It is a brutal business. My friend's only chance to stay and succeed depended on his passion to survive there.

He would need persistence.

Persistence, def: Continuing beyond the usual in spite of opposition, obstacles and discouragement.

This is not just a word in a dictionary; this is a fire that never burns out if you are serious about attaining your goal. Most people do not possess it or let it possess them.

Most people fail when it comes to their dreams. They settle for second best. They quit.

I don't want you to be one of those people.

My friend never considered plan B for his life. It was Hollywood or nothing. He was going to leave his apartment in Georgia and that was it.

Oh, did I tell you he was a newlywed? Did I mention he was married to a dyed-in-the-wool, Georgia girl who had no desire to leave home and head west? She would rather die than live in Tinseltown.

No way.

My friend convinced his wife to let him go audition at the Comedy Store on Sunset Boulevard for a chance to appear on, *The Tonight Show.* She finally relented and said, "Okay, but nothing else after that."

He performed at the club and bombed. Total failure. He sat on the plane in Los Angeles and laughed at his impossible dream. Back in Georgia, he told his wife it had been a disaster.

She smiled knowingly and said, "At least you

tried. I'm proud of you."

Then, he informed her they were moving to Hollywood.

She almost fainted.

A month later, they were on their way west. His wife didn't speak to him for the entire trip. She angrily stared out the car window and thought to herself, "I married a lunatic."

He had no prior television experience so the lunatic sent a demo video to ABC television from a comedy routine he had done at a church youth group. It was a very unprofessional video, to say the least. It was all my friend had to showcase his talent.

Weeks went by. There was no word from ABC.

He wanted to do commercials. He was told to find a photographer and get his head shots done. He spent what little money he and his wife had to do it. He also needed an agent. He couldn't find one.

His young wife was getting restless. She wanted to move back to Georgia.

He had to make her happy so he came up with a temporary fix.

He bought her a horse.

Then, he went back to dreaming.

Everywhere he went he hit a wall. An executive at CBS told him he wasn't funny. NBC blew him off, too. Executives at TBS in Atlanta said they weren't interested. He finally found an agent and went on commercial auditions for a year.

Nothing.

"**Success is stumbling from failure to failure with no loss of enthusiasm.**"
Winston Churchill

He and his wife were eating peanut butter and jelly sandwiches almost every night. They were broke. He was making less than $200.00 a week for a television show he was hosting that aired locally at 6:00 a.m. on Saturday mornings.

His dream had become a joke and his marriage was falling apart. All his friends and family told him to quit and give it up. His reputation as a lunatic had extended to several hundred people now.

He had no contacts, no acting ability, no idea how to get a career started and most of all, no experience.

But, he refused to quit.

He knew who he was and he was not going to give up. He auditioned for, *Happy Days.*

Nope.

Then he read for, *Mork ana Mindy.*

They didn't want him, either.

He figured out ways to get invited to Hollywood parties and met a lot of famous people. They told him to

call them and he did just that. But, no one took his call.
No one called him back.

It slowly began to dawn on him that his dream
was dying. While his wife was out riding her horse, he
got down on his knees on a Sunday afternoon and said a
simple prayer, **"I am not giving up but I need a little
help here, Lord. Please."**

At 7:00 a.m. the ***next*** morning, his phone rang
and he heard a voice screaming into his ear, "We want
YOU!" He groggily mumbled, "Who is this?"

It was ABC Television.

They signed him to a three year deal to be their
comedian for a new show they were producing called,
Kids Are People, Too.

Then, he landed a full-time job for a television
station in Chicago for six figures and wound up as a
successful actor in commercials landing spots for
McDonald's, J.C. Penney, Continental Airlines, CBS
Entertainment and even beating out Jay Leno for a
doughnut commercial.

He also went on to win three Emmy awards for
television excellence.

Not bad for a lunatic, huh?

His prayer had been answered and his
persistence had been rewarded.

My friend had not only found his dream, he found the stars.

"It's supposed to be hard. If it wasn't hard, everyone would do it. The hard... is what makes it great."

Jimmy Dugan (played by Tom Hanks) in the movie, *A League of Their Own*.

You want to see your dream come true?

Here are the steps to help you accomplish it:

Get a dream

Don't just run in the hamster wheel; begin to really pursue the passion for your life.

Let it percolate in your soul

Dreams take time to take hold. Make sure your dream is your heart. If it grows daily inside you, it's your real dream.

Become convinced of it

It may take a couple of years for you to get to the point where you finally *act* on it, but when you do, that is your dream. GO for it with abandon!

Write it down

Writing is believing. When you just think of it in your mind, it is not as powerful or memorable.

Start sharing it with others

By seeing your family members or friends get excited about it, you will gain the emotional and psychological impetus to build your momentum towards fruition. A word of caution: For those people who do not believe you will achieve your dream, drop them like a two-foot putt. You don't need the negativity here. Stay positive!

Deepen your work ethic

Going for your dream is the hardest work you will ever do because you have a high goal here and you are very passionate about it. That will not only take a lot of energy it will tax your emotions, too.

Visualize victory

A great technique that has worked for thousands of Dreamers. Like a quarterback who imagines himself walking off the field after the Super Bowl as the winner, "visualizing victory" works in any field and any challenge. See it in advance and many times it will come true.

Expect failures and setbacks

Dreams are never easy, that's why they are called, "dreams." You want to be challenged, you want to fight and you want to overcome everything and anything to get to the end. Fasten your seat belt and be prepared for the battle of your life. How cool is THAT!

Promise yourself you will never quit

Like, **"The Little Engine that Could,"** you commit yourself to stay chuggin' until you are over that mountain of your Dream!

Stay positive...always

The Dream will require ongoing persistence with a foundation of optimism not pity, sadness or regrets. These are your series of moments to shine. Embrace them. Like an Olympic runner, get off to a good lead and never look back. Smile your way to your Dream. You can do it. You *will* do it!

"The sky is not my limit...I am."
T.F. Hodge, From Within I Rise: Spiritual Triumph Over Death and Conscious Encounters with "The Divine Presence"

At a point in my life, I made a commitment to follow the dream of becoming a championship women's college basketball referee. A Dream like this means you start at the bottom. You have to pursue it with character, passion, a lot of learning, patience and most of all, *persistence.*

It is a commitment of long, lonely hours as you build up game experience and credibility within the sport. I was prepared to reach that mountain of success. I was not going to give up until I realized my goal.

I began officiating basketball in 1988 at a junior high game in Bloomington, Illinois. I was in over my head. I did so many basic things incorrectly.

But, I wanted to be a great referee so I worked hard at my craft. From not knowing where to stand to learning hundreds of rules, those early days were tough for me. I was a struggling referee.

But, I stayed with it.

I kept asking great refs how to do it right. I had a passion for learning the game and most importantly, I loved being a basketball official.

And, a remarkable thing happened.

I got better.

As I advanced into high school games, through junior college and division 3 games, I began to see my dream of becoming a NCAA collegiate referee for women's basketball. I had decided that I **wanted** to do this, really pursue it.

I had a passion to be the best.

"Success doesn't come to you, you go to it."
T. Scott McLeod

It wasn't always easy.

In January of 2001, I was sent on a trip to work a game that was 210 miles each way through a major snow storm. It took me four hours to get there and six hours to get home; I arrived at 2:45 a.m. I spent $100 in gas and got paid $105 to work the game, a five dollar profit.

How did I feel after that experience?

I was thrilled.

When I laid my head down on my pillow that night, I was smiling. I was doing something I loved. As they say, "It doesn't get any better than that!"

Most of my friends asked me, "Why do you do this? You don't make any money? Why spend so many hours in your car to get yelled at for two hours. You're nuts!"

That about sums it up.

I am crazy.

For officiating.

But, it's my passion. Outside of my wife and kids, refereeing is one of the most incredible things I do. I can't get enough of it.

In 2011, my dream came true.

I was honored to work the Division III NCAA Women's Final Four.

That same year I was hired into my first of several Division 1 conferences.

I had the passion and the persistence to realize it. It took me 23 years to find my Impossible Dream. It was worth every minute.

Do what you love and don't ever stop until you get there.

I know.

I did it and so can you.

Believe it.

"I don't believe in destiny, I believe in determination."

A leader loves persistence.

Epilogue

We may have come to the end of this book, yet it is just the beginning of your journey. I hope that journey is one filled with excitement, joy, success and meaning.

This journey is about your *soul*.

Your leadership journey, your progress, your future starts with one word:

Passion

Your life will be a product of what you care about.

What you love, what you spend time on, what you pour your heart into, that is what will be great.

Passion, people, progress.

It all begins with passion.

A *Soul on Fire* is the only flame that can never be put out. It is the fuel to light your future. It is a belief in something so great, so grand and so wonderful that only the best will go for it.

Find your passion.

Share it with the world.

Go ahead, go big.

The world is waiting for you!

Acknowledgements

This book is more than just words to me, it's about my heart, my life, my journey through failure and success, and most importantly, it's about people.

Thank you, the reader, for taking the iniative to get through the book, for dreaming big, and for what you will do to make a difference in the world.

I have been blessed to share life with so many great family, friends, leaders and associates.

I am grateful for every person that has touched my life and influenced me as a person and a leader. We all influence people, and I know that who I am today is a compilation of my life journey and those in it, thank you!

A few specific thanks:

To God, for laying this dream on my heart, for His grace and salvation in life found in Jesus Christ. I am blessed and thankful for my abilities and gifts.

To my mom, you gave up so much of your life so that I would have one. You support all I do and display a passion for love in all you do.

To my brother Steve, for being a great friend, advisor, brother, father, dreamer and friendly Stratego competitor. I can't wait for what's next in our lives.

To Andy Kauffman for setting me on this course.

To Ken Blanchard, Phil Hodges, Phyllis Hendry, Tommy Moore, Karen McGuire, and the entire LLJ team and facilitators; I love your heart, your influence, and the work you do.

To Dan Pongetti for all the great design work, ideas, creativity and the renewing water.

To Pat Hurley, your heart is so big, your love for the dream is real, and you care so much for this journey. I appreciate your words, your ideas, your time, your support, and most of all, your passion.

Finally, to my children, Trevor, Brendon and Nevaeh, you may not realize the influence you have on me every day. You remind me of what life is really all about, on how important my role as a father and leader in our home is, and I thank you for being great people. Follow your passions and the world will love you for it, just as I do.

Randy Fox
January 20, 2014

Presents

Randy Fox
"The World is Waiting for You!"

A dynamic and practical **leadership book series**, along with **keynote messages** and **workshops,** designed to make you think about your potential and to help you realize it.

"Soul on Fire"

A challenge to be a passionate leader using poignant stories, memorable quotes, practical nuggets, humor and inspirational examples from the lives of great leaders. This will get you fired up!

"Refined by Fire"

A how-to motivational message on growing as a leader for maximum impact. Randy gets real with practical principles that refine the way you work and live, including: managing your priorities and ego, finding success from failures, honing your skills, the importance of advisers and more.

"Making Others SMILE!"

Be a leader who turns average employees into stars, helping them succeed beyond their dreams. Randy emphasizes a positive attitude, taking professional and personal risks to improve your status quo situation and the joy of finding your heartfelt passion in life.

Workshops

"Get a LIFE!"

An engaging and interactive session on stress management. Randy uses a *Top Ten* list of suggestions to ease the pressures we face as leaders and people. Highlights include, *Do that off-putting thing, Revisit your childhood, Find a fun soul mate, Reward yourself daily, Find your real passion*, and more.

"How to get along with those who don't *deserve* it!"

An interactive program on the four types of leaders. Your team will laugh out loud as their leadership style is revealed and how it irritates others. The result is a healthy respect for differences in style and a bond that forms within the group as they accept each others' uniqueness. Practical and powerful.

To connect with Randy or learn more about FoxPoint, visit:

http://foxpoint.net

facebook.com/foxpoint

twitter.com/randy_foxpoint

linkedin.com/in/foxrandy

877.411.8498

Also available from Randy Fox

You want to grow, to succeed, and to improve.
Your progress depends on your principles.
Journey with us as we look at the simple, yet
effective and practical things every leader must do
to get ahead.

Order your copy today!   **http://foxpoint.net**